DALLAS
COWBOYS

by J Chris Roselius

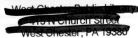

THIS BOOK CONTAINS AT LEAST 10% RECYCLED MATERIALS.

Editor: Chrös McDougall
Copy Editor: Nicholas Cafarelli
Interior Design and Production: Christa Schneider
Cover Design: Christa Schneider

Photo Credits: Amy Gutierrez/AP Images, cover; AP Images, title page, 10, 12, 42 (top); NFL Photos/AP Images, 7, 15, 17, 19, 20, 29, 42 (middle), 42 (bottom), 43 (bottom); Vernon Biever/Getty Images, 4; William Straeter/AP Images, 8; Ron Heflin/AP Images, 23, 43 (top); Tim Sharp/AP Images, 25, 31, 43 (middle); Glenn James/AP Images, 26; Susan Ragan/AP Images, 33; Brett Coomer/AP Images, 34; Tony Gutierrez/AP Images, 37; L. M. Otero/AP Images, 39; James D Smith/AP Images, 41; Paul Spinelli/AP Images, 44; Sharon Ellman/AP Images, 47

Library of Congress Cataloging-in-Publication Data
Roselius, J Chris.
  Dallas Cowboys / J Chris Roselius.
     p. cm. — (Inside the nfl)
  Includes index.
  ISBN 978-1-61714-009-9
  1. Dallas Cowboys (Football team)—History—Juvenile literature. I. Title.
  GV956.D3R65 2011
  796.332'64097642812—dc22
                    2010016176

TABLE OF CONTENTS

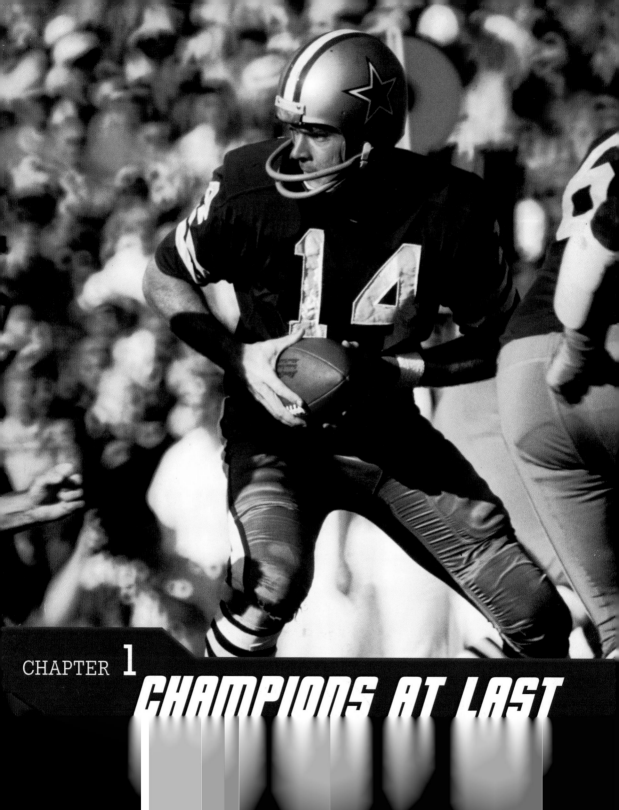

CHAPTER 1

CHAMPIONS AT LAST

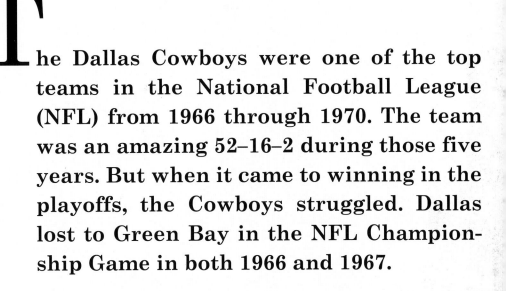

T he Dallas Cowboys were one of the top teams in the National Football League (NFL) from 1966 through 1970. The team was an amazing 52–16–2 during those five years. But when it came to winning in the playoffs, the Cowboys struggled. Dallas lost to Green Bay in the NFL Championship Game in both 1966 and 1967.

Dallas fans believed the Cowboys were finally going to break through in 1970. The Cowboys finished the regular season 10–4. Then they won two playoff games and advanced to Super Bowl V against the Baltimore Colts. But the Cowboys again failed to end their championship drought. The Colts kicked a field goal in the final minute to win 16–13.

The loss was tough for the Cowboys to take. That disappointment seemed to carry

DALLAS QUARTERBACK CRAIG MORTON PREPARES TO HAND OFF THE BALL AGAINST THE BALTIMORE COLTS IN SUPER BOWL V.

into the start of the 1971 season. After winning its first two games, Dallas then lost three of its next five. The Cowboys had a 4–3 record halfway through the season.

But the Cowboys started to turn their season around. On November 7 they beat the St. Louis Cardinals 16–13. That sparked a seven-game winning streak. The Cowboys finished the regular season 11–3. They went on to beat the Minnesota Vikings 20–12 in the first round of the playoffs. Then they beat the San Francisco 49ers 14–3 in the National Football Conference

(NFC) Championship Game. They advanced to their second straight Super Bowl.

Super Bowl VI was in New Orleans, Louisiana. The Cowboys' opponent was the American Football Conference (AFC) champion Miami Dolphins. Dallas fans were nervous before the game. They had seen their team come up short in too many title games before. But this Cowboys team proved to be like no other before them. From the start of the game, the Cowboys dominated the Dolphins.

Dallas' offense racked up 23 first downs in the game. It gained 352 yards. The defense held Miami to only 10 first downs and 185 total yards. Dallas never trailed in the game.

They jumped out to a 3–0 lead at the end of the first quarter and held a 10–3 lead at the

QUARTERBACK ROGER STAUBACH LOOKS TO PASS OVER A LEAPING MIAMI DOLPHINS DEFENDER DURING SUPER BOWL VI.

half. The Cowboys then scored one touchdown in the third and another one in the fourth quarter. Meanwhile, the defense did not allow the Dolphins to score a single point. The Cowboys won 24–3. Years of playoff frustrations were over.

Leading the charge for the Cowboys on offense were quarterback Roger Staubach and running back Duane Thomas.

Staubach ran the offense to near perfection. He completed 12 of his 19 passes for 119 yards and two touchdowns. He earned the Most Valuable Player (MVP) award. Meanwhile, Thomas slashed his way through the Miami offense for 95 rushing yards and a touchdown on 19 carries.

But the offense was only half the story. It was the Cowboys' defense that shut down the Miami offense all day. The Dolphins became the first team in Super Bowl history to not score a touchdown.

Linebacker Chuck Howley and defensive tackle Bob Lilly were the stars. Lilly completely dominated Miami's offensive line. He even recorded a sack of

DALLAS RUNNING BACK DUANE THOMAS RUSHED FOR 95 YARDS AND A TOUCHDOWN ON 19 CARRIES IN SUPER BOWL VI.

The Cowboys were finally champions. The team could forget about its challenging first six years as a franchise from 1960 to 1965. Instead, the Cowboys were on the verge of becoming known as "America's Team."

Miami quarterback Bob Griese for a Super Bowl-record 29-yard loss in the first quarter.

Howley was even more effective. He recovered a fumble in the first quarter to set up a Cowboys field goal. He added an interception in the fourth quarter that he returned 41 yards. The interception set up a Staubach touchdown pass to tight end Mike Ditka for the game's final score.

COWBOYS COACH TOM LANDRY IS CARRIED OFF THE FIELD AFTER DALLAS DEFEATED THE MIAMI DOLPHINS 24–3 IN SUPER BOWL VI.

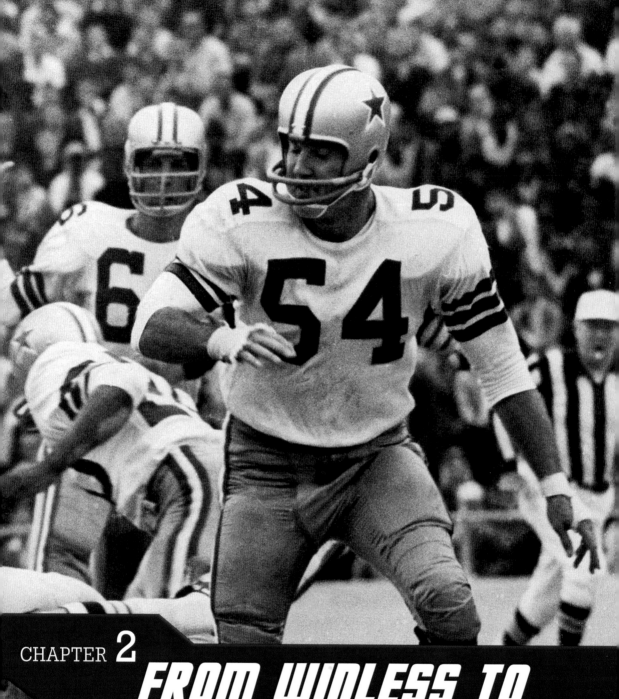

FROM WINLESS TO AMERICA'S TEAM

The Dallas Cowboys came into existence on January 28, 1960. That is when the NFL awarded an expansion franchise to Clint Murchison Jr. and Bedford Wynne. Murchison was the majority owner. That meant he owned most of the team. The team was first known as the Steers and then the Rangers before the owners settled on the Cowboys.

The Cowboys had only a few months to put a team together before their first game that fall. Murchison, however, had already lined up some people in the front office. The most notable were general manager Tex Schramm, director of player personnel Gil Brandt, and coach Tom Landry. All three would hold their jobs for 29 years.

The Cowboys stocked their roster through an expansion draft. During that draft, they selected three players off the rosters of the existing 12 NFL teams. The rest of the roster

CHUCK HOWLEY (54) PREPARES TO ATTEMPT A TACKLE DURING A 1964 GAME AGAINST THE CLEVELAND BROWNS.

was pieced together by signing players without contracts and through trades with other teams. They were able to trade their future draft picks as well as the players they already obtained. However, the Cowboys were not able to build through the NFL Draft. They entered the league too late to participate.

ALL ABOUT THE NAME

When Clint Murchison was trying to come up with a team name, his first selection was the Steers. He then chose the Dallas Rangers. That was the same nickname of the minor league franchise that was expected to leave the city. However, the Rangers never left and so Murchison settled on Cowboys.

Except for a few players, the team lacked a lot of talent. That showed on the field. The Cowboys did not win a game their first season, going 0–11–1. In fact, the team would struggle to win at all during its first five years of existence. Its best record was 5–8–1, which happened in both 1962 and 1964.

Under the steady leadership of Schramm, Brandt, and Landry, Dallas slowly added talented players. They had started with skilled quarterback Don Meredith and running back Don Perkins in 1960. Then they added defensive tackle Bob Lilly in 1961, linebacker Lee Roy Jordan in 1963, and quarterback Roger Staubach, defensive back Mel Renfro, and wide receiver Bob Hayes in 1964.

Still, the Cowboys' record over their first five years was 18–46–4. But that finally began to change in 1965. With loads of young but talented players, Dallas went 7–7. The Cowboys would not experience another losing season until 1986. During that 20-season winning streak, the Cowboys also qualified for

COWBOYS RUNNING BACK DON PERKINS CUTS THROUGH A GAP AGAINST THE WASHINGTON REDSKINS IN 1967.

the playoffs in 17 of the 18 years from 1966 through 1983.

Meredith was leading the offense in 1966. Dallas won its first Eastern Conference title that season. However, they lost to the Green Bay Packers 34–27 in the NFL Championship Game.

CAPTAIN COMEBACK

The Cowboys drafted quarterback Roger Staubach in the 1964 NFL Draft. After a five-year commitment to the U.S. Naval Academy, he finally arrived in Dallas in 1969. There, he would lead the team to one of the greatest stretches of success that any franchise has ever experienced.

Staubach was a Pro Bowl selection six times and NFL passing champion four times. He guided the Cowboys to two Super Bowl titles and earned the MVP honors of Super Bowl VI. He also ranks second in club history with 22,700 yards passing.

He became known as "Captain Comeback." That was because he led 23 game-winning drives. One of his most famous passes was a 50-yard "Hail Mary" touchdown pass to Drew Pearson in the 1975 playoffs to defeat the Minnesota Vikings.

Staubach retired after the 1979 season. In 1985, he was enshrined in the Pro Football Hall of Fame.

Dallas advanced to the NFL Championship Game again in 1967 and again lost to Green Bay, this time 21–17. That second game is now known as the "Ice Bowl" because it was played in below-zero temperatures on a frozen field in Green Bay, Wisconsin.

Beginning in 1967, the NFL Championship Game determined who would play the winner from the American Football League (AFL) in what is now known as the Super Bowl. After beating Dallas, Green Bay went on to beat the Kansas City Chiefs in Super Bowl I.

From 1966 to 1969, the Cowboys went 42–12–2. And they were only getting warmed up. During the 1970s, Dallas went to a record five Super Bowls. The Cowboys won the title after the 1971 season

COWBOYS RUNNING BACK TONY DORSETT RAN FOR 66 YARDS AND A
TOUCHDOWN AS A ROOKIE IN SUPER BOWL XII.

against the Miami Dolphins. They also won the title after the 1977 season against the Denver Broncos. However, they lost the Super Bowl after the 1970 season to the Baltimore Colts and after the 1975 and 1978 seasons to the Pittsburgh Steelers.

Leading the charge in the 1970s was a collection of future Hall of Fame players. They included Staubach and running back Tony Dorsett. Both players starred when the Cowboys beat the Broncos 27–10 in Super Bowl XII. Staubach completed

17 of 25 passes for 183 yards in the game. The rookie Dorsett scored the first touchdown of the game. Despite having to leave the game in the third quarter with an injury, he still ran for 66 yards on 15 carries.

The Cowboys' defense had shut down opposing offenses all season. That is just what they did to Denver in the Super Bowl. The defense led by safety Cliff Harris and defensive tackle Randy White was one of the best every year during the decade. In Super Bowl XII, the Cowboys limited the Broncos to 156 total yards.

The Cowboys were on top of the NFL world during the 1970s. After the 1978 season, NFL Films was putting together a highlight video. The film crew wanted a catchy name for the video, so editor-in-chief Bob Ryan called the Cowboys "America's Team." It is a nickname that has stayed with the team to this day.

HE SAID IT

"*We should have won Super Bowl XIII. We felt going into that game that we were a better team than the Pittsburgh Steelers, and we were devastated by that loss, really. It took a lot out of us. We wanted to be regarded as one of those unique teams that won back-to-back Super Bowls, but we just made too many mistakes in that game, just didn't have enough time at the end to beat the Steelers, but we should have beat them.*" —Receiver Drew Pearson talking about losing Super Bowl XIII to Pittsburgh 35–31

The Cowboys lost to the Pittsburgh Steelers in Super Bowl XIII after the 1978 season. It would be a while before the Cowboys could again live up to their lofty nickname.

THE COWBOYS DEFENSE FLUSTERED THE DENVER BRONCOS IN SUPER BOWL XII, ALLOWING ONLY 156 TOTAL YARDS IN THE GAME.

CHAPTER 3

FALLING ON HARD TIMES

After their Super Bowl XIII loss to the Pittsburgh Steelers, the Cowboys would not return to the Super Bowl for 14 years. The Cowboys underwent a lot of change during the 1980s. One of the biggest changes came in 1984 when Clint Murchison Jr. sold the team to H. R. "Bum" Bright. Only five years later, Bright sold the team to Jerry Jones.

In 1980, Danny White took over at quarterback for the retired Roger Staubach. Dallas finished 12–4 in each of his first two seasons. They went 6–3 in the strike-shortened 1982 season. In 1983, White again led the Cowboys to a 12–4 record.

TONY DORSETT

Tony Dorsett finished his career with 12,739 yards and was a four-time Pro Bowl selection. His most famous run came on January 3, 1983. He took a handoff from Danny White and raced 99 yards for a touchdown. That set an NFL record that can be matched but can never be broken. He entered the Pro Football Hall of Fame in 1994.

COWBOYS QUARTERBACK DANNY WHITE ROLLS OUT AND LOOKS DOWNFIELD AGAINST THE TAMPA BAY BUCCANEERS IN 1980.

COACH LANDRY

For 29 years, Tom Landry was the only head coach the Dallas Cowboys had ever known. During that time, he had a record of 270–178–6 (including playoffs). Only two coaches have won more games. Landry also led the Cowboys to five Super Bowl appearances during the 1970s, winning twice. He won five NFC titles and 13 division titles. The franchise had 20 straight winning seasons under his leadership.

As a defensive coach for the New York Giants in the 1950s, Landry helped develop the 4-3 defense. That scheme had four down linemen and three linebackers. Many teams still use that formation today. As Dallas's coach, Landry introduced offensive motion, reintroduced the shotgun formation, used situational substitutions, and created the flex defense.

Landry was inducted into the Pro Football Hall of Fame in 1990. Landry, who was a native Texan, died on February 12, 2000, of leukemia.

But White never could get the Cowboys to the Super Bowl. Because of that, he never won the hearts of the Dallas fans in the way that Staubach did. In 10 playoff games from 1980 to 1985, White's Cowboys were only 5–5.

The 1985 season was the last winning season for legendary coach Tom Landry. The Cowboys dropped to 7–9 in 1986. It was their first losing season since 1964. Things did not get much better the following year. Dallas went 7–8. Then, the Cowboys collapsed. In 1988 they suffered their worst season since 1960 as they fell to 3–13.

Landry had been the only coach the Cowboys ever had. But Jones fired him after the 1988 season. Landry had an emotional meeting with the players a few days later.

COWBOYS OWNER JERRY JONES, SHOWN IN 1995, BOUGHT THE TEAM IN 1989. HE FIRED HEAD COACH TOM LANDRY SHORTLY AFTER.

However, in typical Landry fashion, he exited with class.

"The way you react to adversity is the key to success," he told his players. "Right now, the situation around here is in turmoil and how we react will be important . . . important in how the season goes next year. I don't want anyone to concern themselves with what has happened to me, but to look forward to playing in September."

Before long, Tex Schramm and Gil Brandt were gone, too. Jones made it clear that he was in charge. He hired Jimmy Johnson to replace Landry without Schramm knowing. Seeing that he was no longer welcomed,

Schramm retired. Brandt stayed a little longer to help with the upcoming draft. But soon after that, Brandt was gone as well. In a matter of months, three people who had been cornerstones of the team were no longer members of the Dallas Cowboys.

Jones's handling of Landry, Brandt, and Schramm was unpopular in Dallas. But Jones had a plan, and he was going to stick with it. Johnson had been a successful coach at the University of Miami. Both Johnson and Jones shared the same vision. They believed that it was time for a change. It was out with the old and in with the new.

One of the new players was wide receiver Michael Irvin. The team had drafted Irvin in 1988. He went on to have 32 catches for 654 yards and five touchdowns during his rookie season. The Cowboys had still finished with the worst record in the league in 1988. That meant they had the first pick in the 1989 NFL Draft. Jones and Johnson wanted a new leader. They also wanted a player who they felt could take advantage of Irvin's talents. The player they targeted was Troy Aikman. That selection helped return the Cowboys to glory.

TEX SCHRAMM

Earnest "Tex" Schramm joined the Cowboys as the team's first president and general manager. Dallas went to five Super Bowls and compiled an NFL-record 20 straight winning seasons during his time. Schramm also helped create the traditional Cowboys home game each Thanksgiving Day. He helped bring the use of instant replay to help officials during a game. Schramm was also part of creating the wild-card playoff system. He even created the Dallas Cowboys Cheerleaders, who were the first of their kind in professional football.

THE DALLAS COWBOYS DRAFTED WIDE RECEIVER MICHAEL IRVIN WITH THE ELEVENTH PICK IN THE 1988 NFL DRAFT.

CHAPTER 4

THE TRADE AND THE TRIPLETS

The Jimmy Johnson era did not start well in Dallas. The young coach had to decide on a starting quarterback. He decided on the rookie, Troy Aikman. He also picked a host of other young and inexperienced players for the starting lineup. The result was not good. The Cowboys went 1–15. Their only win came against the Washington Redskins.

The team made a decision late in the 1989 season that would dramatically change its course. When it became clear that the Cowboys were not going to have a good season, Jerry Jones decided to make a big trade. The Cowboys organized a move that would send star running back Herschel Walker to the Minnesota Vikings. In return, the Cowboys would receive several high draft picks spread over three years.

The trade was supposed to put the Vikings over the edge

QUARTERBACK TROY AIKMAN STARTED DURING HIS ROOKIE SEASON IN 1989. IT WAS ALSO COACH JIMMY JOHNSON'S FIRST SEASON.

ROBO QB

Troy Aikman's professional career did not get off to a great start. He was thrown into the starting lineup as a rookie. Aikman lost his first 11 games and led the Cowboys to a 1–15 record in 1989. But Aikman would go on to become one of the greatest quarterbacks the franchise has ever seen.

He guided the Cowboys to four straight appearances in the NFC Championship Game and won three Super Bowl titles. He won 90 games during the 1990s, becoming the win-ningest quarterback of any decade.

By the time he retired, Aikman racked up 47 different passing records for Dallas. They included completions (2,898), passing yards (32,942), and touchdown passes (165). Aikman was selected to six straight Pro Bowls. He was inducted into the Pro Football Hall of Fame in 2006. After his playing days were over, Aikman went on to a successful broadcasting career.

by giving them a star player. Instead, it was the Cowboys who came out ahead—way ahead. The Cowboys used those picks to build a new core of star players. Some of the players they selected with those picks were running back Emmitt Smith, defensive tackle Russell Maryland, cornerback Kevin Smith, strong safety Darren Woodson, as well as cornerback Clayton Holmes.

The addition of Smith to Aikman and Michael Irvin helped turn the Cowboys into an offensive power. The three players soon became known as the "Triplets." Smith rushed for 937 yards and 11 touch-downs during his rookie season in 1990. Meanwhile, Aikman threw for 2,579 yards and 11 touchdowns. Irvin, however, missed the first month of the season due to a knee injury.

EMMITT SMITH RAN FOR 132 YARDS AND TWO TOUCHDOWNS IN SUPER BOWL XVIII. HE WAS NAMED THE SUPER BOWL MVP.

He finished with 413 receiving yards and five touchdowns. But the team had vastly improved and finished 7–9. The Cowboys would improve even more in the years to come.

Behind Aikman, Smith, and Irvin, the Cowboys were soon dominant. They finished the 1992 season 13–3. After two more victories, the Cowboys were back in the Super Bowl. Aikman threw four touchdown passes against the AFC champion Buffalo Bills. The Cowboys demolished the Bills to win Super Bowl XXVII by a score of 52–17. Aikman was named MVP of the game.

The Cowboys were back one year later. They had dominated opponents in a 12–4 regular season. After two playoff victories, they met the Bills again in Super Bowl XXVIII. The result was the same. Smith ran for 132 yards and two touchdowns to earn MVP honors. The Cowboys beat the Bills 30–13.

KING OF RUNNING

Emmitt Smith was a star running back at the University of Florida. But many pro scouts did not believe he was big enough to handle the punishment that NFL running backs receive. After 15 years in the NFL—13 of which were with Dallas—Smith retired as the league's all-time leading rusher in both yards and touchdowns. He had 18,355 career rushing yards and 164 career touchdowns. Smith was selected to the Pro Bowl eight times. In 1993, two major press organizations named him the league's MVP. Smith was selected to the Pro Bowl eight times. He was inducted into the Pro Football Hall of Fame in 2010.

"It's too early to call us the Team of the Nineties," Aikman said after the game. "But I guess this says last year was not a fluke. It puts us with some great teams. What exactly that means to all of us, I'm not sure.

"Last year's Super Bowl was one of disbelief, a bunch of young, bright-eyed guys caught up in it all. This is one of satisfaction because the expectations were so much higher."

Aikman, Smith, and Irvin were spectacular during Dallas's back-to-back title seasons. Aikman threw for a combined 6,545 yards and 38 touchdowns while giving up only 20 interceptions. He completed an amazing 69.1 percent of his passes in 1993. Smith led the NFL in rushing from 1991 to 1993 and again in 1995. That included a 1,713-yard, 18-touchdown season in 1992. Meanwhile, Irvin had five

TROY AIKMAN, *LEFT*, EMMITT SMITH, *CENTER*, AND MICHAEL IRVIN, *RIGHT*, WERE KNOWN AS THE "TRIPLETS."

straight 1,000-plus yard seasons from 1991 to 1995. He averaged 1,418.6 yards and 89.8 receptions per season.

Johnson had a falling out with Jones after the 1993 season. That led to Johnson resigning as the team's coach. Jones brought in former University of Oklahoma coach Barry Switzer. Thanks in large part to the "Triplets," the Cowboys hardly skipped a beat.

Dallas went 12–4 during Switzer's first season in 1994. But they were denied a chance to win their third straight Super Bowl. The Cowboys lost 38–28 to the San Francisco 49ers in the NFC Championship Game.

However, they were back again one year later. The Cowboys went 12–4 in the regular season. This time, they reached the Super Bowl. They defeated the Pittsburgh Steelers 27–17 in Super Bowl XXX.

Cornerback Larry Brown had a big game for Dallas. He came away with two interceptions. He returned his first interception 44 yards to the Pittsburgh 18. That set up Smith's 1-yard touchdown run to give the Cowboys a 20–7 lead.

The second came in the fourth quarter and helped the Cowboys seal the win. The Steelers had cut the deficit to 20–17. But Brown came up with his second interception. He returned it

THE PLAYMAKER

Michael Irvin retired after the 1999 season due to a spine injury. He left the Cowboys owning or sharing 20 team receiving records. They included career receptions (750), career yardage (11,904), and 100-yard receiving games (47). When he retired, only two NFL receivers had more 1,000-yard receiving seasons than Irvin's seven. Jerry Rice had 12 and Steve Largent had eight. In 1995, Irvin had a record 11 100-yard receiving games. His seven consecutive 100-yard games that season is an NFL record as well. He was inducted into the Pro Football Hall of Fame in 2007.

33 yards to set up Smith's 4-yard touchdown run.

"I made a great break on the ball," Brown said. "The slant was coming, and I beat the receiver to it. They try to throw everything on timing, and I was just able to get there first."

Brown's elite performance and the Cowboys' fifth Super Bowl title would cap an unbelievable four-year run by the team. Switzer would last only

CORNERBACK LARRY BROWN WAS NAMED SUPER BOWL XXX MVP IN 1996. HE INTERCEPTED TWO PASSES IN THE WIN AGAINST PITTSBURGH.

two more seasons with Dallas. He was fired in 1997 after a 6–10 season. Chan Gailey was hired to try to lift the Cowboys back to the Super Bowl. But he lasted only two seasons. The Cowboys entered the new decade on a downward slide, still seeking a sixth Super Bowl title.

PRIME TIME

Dallas signed Deion Sanders before the 1995 season. Sanders was a star cornerback. But he also played wide receiver at times and returned kicks and punts. Sanders also played for four different Major League Baseball teams. He even played in the 1992 World Series with the Atlanta Braves. Sanders helped the Cowboys win Super Bowl XXX. He played in Dallas from 1995 to 1999 and was known as one of the top defensive players in the league.

CHAPTER 5

TRYING TO GET BACK

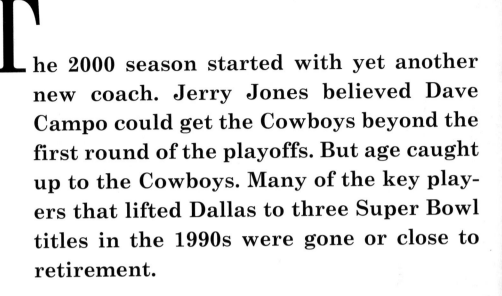

The 2000 season started with yet another new coach. Jerry Jones believed Dave Campo could get the Cowboys beyond the first round of the playoffs. But age caught up to the Cowboys. Many of the key players that lifted Dallas to three Super Bowl titles in the 1990s were gone or close to retirement.

Michael Irvin retired after the 1999 season. Troy Aikman's last season came in 2000. Running back Emmitt Smith was still a key member of the team. But he was no longer the dominant running back he was five years earlier. The loss of talent on the field showed in the stand-

ings. The Cowboys were 5–11 in Campo's first season.

The Cowboys struggled to find a replacement for Aikman. They posted 5–11 records during each of the next two seasons as well. Quincy Carter saw most of the playing time as quarterback in 2001 and 2002. But Anthony

QUARTERBACK QUINCY CARTER DROPS BACK AND LOOKS TO PASS DURING A GAME AGAINST THE HOUSTON TEXANS IN 2002.

Wright, Ryan Leaf, and Clint Stoerner all took snaps for the Cowboys in 2001. Carter split time with Chad Hutchinson in 2002.

One of the few highlights in 2002 came on October 27. The Cowboys were playing the Seattle Seahawks at Texas Stadium. On an 11-yard run that day, Smith became the NFL's all-time leading rusher. He moved past Walter Payton's mark of 16,726 career rushing yards. Smith finished the day with 109 yards on 24 carries. At season's end, he had extended the record to 17,162 career rushing yards.

"[Sunday] is a special day for me, my family and the Payton family," Smith said after the game. "Because without Payton doing what he did in the National Football League and representing all he represented, he wouldn't have given a young man like myself a dream, something to shoot after and a person to look up to and try to emulate in every way possible."

Campo was fired after the 2002 season. Jones named Bill Parcells the new coach. Parcells had won two Super Bowls with the New York Giants. He quickly turned the Cowboys around. He showed faith in Carter in 2003. The young quarterback responded by throwing for 3,302 yards and 17 touchdowns. Carter led Dallas to a 10–6 record. It was the team's first winning season since 1998. But the Cowboys again lost in the first round of the playoffs. They lost to the Carolina Panthers in the wild-card game.

RUNNING BACK EMMITT SMITH HOLDS UP A TROPHY AFTER SURPASSING WALTER PAYTON AS THE NFL'S ALL-TIME LEADING RUSHER IN 2002.

AN UNLIKELY STAR

Tony Romo played his college football at Eastern Illinois University in Division II. No teams took a chance on him in the NFL Draft. The Cowboys instead signed him as a free agent.

Romo was a backup for his first three seasons. He did not start until October 29, 2006, against Carolina. By the end of the year, his performance was so impressive that he became Dallas's first Pro Bowl quarterback since Troy Aikman in 1996. In 2007, he guided the Cowboys to a 13–3 record, tying the franchise record for most regular season wins.

During his short career, Romo has set single-season club records for touchdown passes (36), completions (347), yards (4,483), and 300-yard passing games (eight). From 2006 to 2007, he threw at least one touchdown pass in 17 straight games, setting another Cowboys record.

Dallas took a step backward in 2004. They went 6–10 as the quarterback carousel continued. Out went Carter and in came Vinny Testaverde. The new quarterback threw for 3,532 yards and 17 touchdowns. But Testaverde lasted only one season. Drew Bledsoe was brought in to lead the team in 2005. He threw for 3,639 yards and 23 touchdowns. But Dallas went 9–7 and failed to make the playoffs.

Bledsoe began the 2006 season as the starter. However, Parcells switched to previously undrafted Tony Romo midway through. With Romo leading the offense, the Cowboys finished with a 6–4 run. They ended the year with a 9–7 record and a date in the playoffs.

QUARTERBACK TONY ROMO ROLLS OUT OF THE POCKET AND LOOKS TO PASS AGAINST THE NEW YORK GIANTS IN 2006.

The Cowboys lost again in the wild-card game. But the future finally looked bright for the team. Romo threw for 2,903 yards and 19 touchdowns in his 12 games. He blossomed in 2007. Romo threw for 4,211 yards and 36 touchdowns to lead Dallas to a 13–3 record in coach Wade Phillips' first year.

Romo continued his impressive play the next two seasons. In 2008, he threw for 3,448 yards and 26 touchdowns in only 13 games. Then he threw for 4,483 yards and 26 touchdowns with only nine interceptions in 2009. The Cowboys went 11–5 and won the NFC Eastern Division title. The Cowboys finally won a first-round playoff game, too. They beat the Philadelphia Eagles 34–14 in the wild-card game. It was their first postseason win since 1996.

That was as far as the Cowboys would go in 2009, however. They lost to the Minnesota Vikings and their star quarterback, Brett Favre, in the second round.

The Cowboys had again failed to reach the Super Bowl. But they had finally turned the corner in 2009. Romo was at the age when many quarterbacks hit their prime. He had finally shown that he could win in a big game. He also developed a connection with up-and-coming receiver Miles Austin.

RECEIVER MILES AUSTIN LOOKS FOR RUNNING ROOM AFTER CATCHING A PASS AGAINST THE SAN FRANCISCO 49ERS IN 2009.

With Romo and Austin leading the offense and linebacker DeMarcus Ware leading an aggressive defense, the Cowboys could once again live up to their nickname as "America's Team."

A NEW HOME

In 2009, the Dallas Cowboys opened the new $1.2 billion Cowboys Stadium. They had previously played in Texas Stadium for 38 seasons. The new stadium is one of the largest domed structures in the world. It features a retractable roof as well as massive high-definition TV screens that hang over the center of the field.

TIMELINE

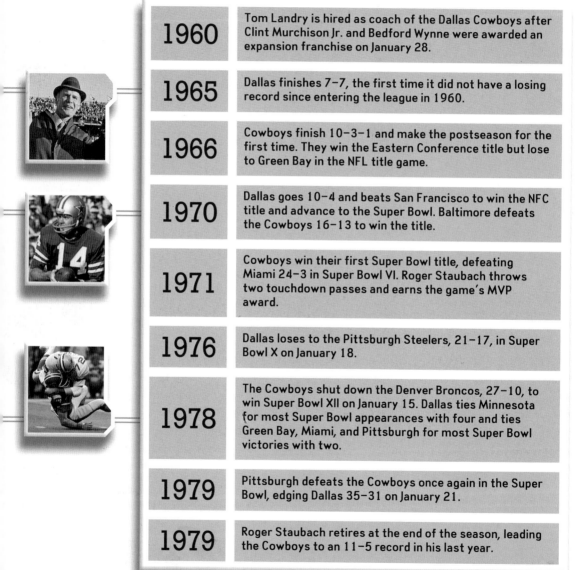

1960	Tom Landry is hired as coach of the Dallas Cowboys after Clint Murchison Jr. and Bedford Wynne were awarded an expansion franchise on January 28.
1965	Dallas finishes 7–7, the first time it did not have a losing record since entering the league in 1960.
1966	Cowboys finish 10–3–1 and make the postseason for the first time. They win the Eastern Conference title but lose to Green Bay in the NFL title game.
1970	Dallas goes 10–4 and beats San Francisco to win the NFC title and advance to the Super Bowl. Baltimore defeats the Cowboys 16–13 to win the title.
1971	Cowboys win their first Super Bowl title, defeating Miami 24–3 in Super Bowl VI. Roger Staubach throws two touchdown passes and earns the game's MVP award.
1976	Dallas loses to the Pittsburgh Steelers, 21–17, in Super Bowl X on January 18.
1978	The Cowboys shut down the Denver Broncos, 27–10, to win Super Bowl XII on January 15. Dallas ties Minnesota for most Super Bowl appearances with four and ties Green Bay, Miami, and Pittsburgh for most Super Bowl victories with two.
1979	Pittsburgh defeats the Cowboys once again in the Super Bowl, edging Dallas 35–31 on January 21.
1979	Roger Staubach retires at the end of the season, leading the Cowboys to an 11–5 record in his last year.

1988	After a 3–13 season, Tom Landry is fired by new team owner Jerry Jones.
1993	The Dallas Cowboys win their third Super Bowl title, defeating Buffalo 52–17 in Super Bowl XXVII on January 31.
1994	The Cowboys repeat as Super Bowl champions on January 30, again beating Buffalo, this time by a score of 31–13.

1996	The Cowboys win their third Super Bowl title in four years on January 28, beating Pittsburgh 27–17. Dallas becomes the first team in NFL history to win three Super Bowls in four years.
2000	Dave Campo is named the new coach, replacing Chan Gailey, who coached the team for only two years.
2001	Troy Aikman announces his retirement on April 9 after 12 years with the Cowboys. Aikman held or tied 47 different club records at the time of his retirement.

2002	Smith bursts up the middle on an 11-yard run against the Seahawks to become the NFL's all-time leading rusher.
2006	Bill Parcells, coach of the Cowboys for three seasons, retires from the coaching profession after the Cowboys lose to Seattle in an NFC wild-card playoff game.
2009	The Cowboys move into their new home, the $1.2 billion Cowboys Stadium. Dallas wins its first playoff game since 1996 when it defeats the Philadelphia Eagles in the first round.

QUICK STATS

FRANCHISE HISTORY

1960–

SUPER BOWLS
(wins in bold)

1970 (V), **1971 (VI)**, 1975 (X), **1977 (XII)**, 1978 (XIII), **1992 (XXVII)**, **1993 (XXVIII)**, **1995 (XXX)**

NFC CHAMPIONSHIP GAMES
(since 1970 AFL-NFL merger)

1970, 1971, 1972, 1973, 1975, 1977, 1978, 1980, 1981, 1982, 1992, 1993, 1994, 1995

DIVISION CHAMPIONSHIPS
(since 1970 AFL-NFL merger)

1970, 1971, 1973, 1976, 1977, 1978, 1979, 1981, 1985, 1992, 1993, 1994, 1995, 1996, 1998, 2007, 2009

KEY PLAYERS
(position, seasons with team)

Troy Aikman (QB, 1989–2000)
Tony Dorsett (RB, 1977–1987)
Bob Hayes (WR, 1965–1974)
Chuck Howley (LB, 1961–1973)
Michael Irvin (WR, 1988–1999)
Bob Lilly (DT, 1961–1974)
Mel Renfro (DB, 1964–1977)
Tony Romo (QB, 2004–)
Emmitt Smith (RB, 1990–2002)
Roger Staubach (QB, 1969–1979)
DeMarcus Ware (LB, 2005–)
Randy White (DT, 1975–1988)
Rayfield Wright (T/TE, 1967–1979)

KEY COACHES

Tom Landry (1960–1988): 250–162–6; 20–16 (playoffs)
Jimmy Johnson (1989–1993): 44–36; 7–1 (playoffs)
Barry Switzer (1994–1997): 40–24; 5–2 (playoffs)

HOME FIELDS

Cowboys Stadium (2009–)
Texas Stadium (1971–2008)
Cotton Bowl (1960–1971)

* All statistics through 2009 season

QUOTES AND ANECDOTES

"He didn't look that big, and he didn't look that fast either, but I've never seen a guy take a football and do any more with it than what he did." — Steve Kiner talking about former Cowboys teammate Duane Thomas.

Mike Ditka not only won a Super Bowl ring with the Cowboys, but he also guided the Chicago Bears to a Super Bowl title as coach in 1985. Ditka is one of three people to win a Super Bowl title as a head coach and a player. The others are Tom Flores and Tony Dungy.

"Tony Dorsett made a big difference when he came in '77. Getting Dorsett was a real shot in the arm. This guy was a sensational player. He had speed, he was tough, could run inside. He took a lot of pressure off me. With him we had a very balanced game. That year Tony Hill also came, and when you have Tony and Drew [Pearson] and Tony, we were one heck of an offense." — Former Dallas quarterback Roger Staubach talking about his former teammate, running back Tony Dorsett.

"I was thinking about quitting coaching altogether and going into business. When Clint and Tex called, I told my wife, 'Well, we might as well take a shot.' The thing was, I wasn't so sure that the Cowboys were going to last more than a couple of years in Dallas. I lived here, and Dallas was a city that didn't turn out unless you won. If you didn't win (the fans) said, 'We'll go do something else.' And I knew we wouldn't win for a while as an expansion team. But it came down to figuring. 'Why not just take a shot?'" — Tom Landry, explaining his thought process when he was asked by owner Clint Murchison and general manager Tex Schramm to become the first head coach of the Cowboys.

GLOSSARY

comeback

Coming from behind to take a lead in a particular game.

contract

A binding agreement about, for example, years of commitment by a football player in exchange for a given salary.

dominant

The player or team that proves to be consistently better than an opponent.

draft

A system used by professional sports leagues to select new players in order to spread incoming talent among all teams.

expansion

In sports, to add a franchise or franchises to a league.

flex defense

A defensive system in which the defensive linemen line up in different areas based on what the other team's offense might try.

Hail Mary

A long and high pass made out of desperation to try to score a touchdown; usually made at the end of a game.

legendary

Well known and admired over a long period.

leukemia

A form of cancer that affects white and red blood cells.

offensive motion

When one or more players shift their position before a play starts, either by taking a few steps to one side or the other or running to the other side of the field.

rookie

A first-year professional athlete.

shotgun formation

An offensive formation in which the quarterback lines up three or four yards behind the center to allow him more time to pass.

FOR MORE INFORMATION

Further Reading

Eisenberg, John. *Cotton Bowl Days: Growing up with Dallas and the Cowboys in the 1960s*. New York: Simon & Schuster, 1997

Housewright, Ed. *100 Things Cowboys Fans Should Know & Do Before They Die*. Chicago: Triumph Books, 2008.

St. Angelo, Ron. *Greatest Team Ever: The Dallas Cowboys Dynasty of the 1990s*. Nashville, TN: Thomas Nelson, 2007.

Web Links

To learn more about the Dallas Cowboys, visit ABDO Publishing Company online at **www.abdopublishing.com**. Web sites about the Cowboys are featured on our Book Links page. These links are routinely monitored and updated to provide the most current information available.

Places to Visit

Cowboys Stadium
900 E. Randol Mill Road
Arlington, TX 76001
817-892-4161
Tours of Cowboys Stadium allow fans behind-the-scenes access to several areas, including the Cowboys Locker Room, Cheerleaders Locker Room, Playing Field, Private Clubs, Media Interview Room, and other areas.

Pro Football Hall of Fame
2121 George Halas Dr., NW
Canton, OH 44708
330-456-8207
www.profootballhof.com
This hall of fame and museum highlights the greatest players and moments in the history of the National Football League. Eighteen people affiliated with the Cowboys are enshrined, including Tony Dorsett, Tom Landry, Emmitt Smith, and Roger Staubach.

INDEX

About the Author

J Chris Roselius has been an award-winning writer and journalist for more than 15 years. A graduate of the University of Texas, he has written numerous books. Currently residing in Houston, Texas, he enjoys spending time with his wife and two children. When not attending baseball games with them, he also likes to watch a variety of sports, on either the professional or collegiate level. In addition, he enjoys traveling, watching history and science programs, and reading the newspaper.